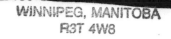

Great Earth Science Projects™

Hands-on Projects About

Weather and Climate

Krista West

The Rosen Publishing Group's
PowerKids Press™
New York

Some of the projects in this book were designed for a child to do together with an adult.

Published in 2002 by The Rosen Publishing Group, Inc.
29 East 21st Street, New York, NY 10010

First Edition

Book Design: Michael de Guzman
Project Editors: Jennifer Landau, Jason Moring, Jennifer Quasha

Photo Credits: p. 4 (rain) © Wolfgang Kaehler/CORBIS, (hail) © David Muench/CORBIS, and (snow) © Michael S. Yamashita/CORBIS; pp 6-21 by Cindy Reiman; pp. 20, 21 (growth rings) © Hans Pfletschinder/Peter Arnold, Inc.; p. 21 (tree) © Ray Pfortner/Peter Arnold, Inc.

West, Krista.
Hands on projects about weather and climate / Krista West.
    p. cm. — (Great earth science projects)
Includes bibliographical references and index.
ISBN 0-8239-5845-0
1. Meteorology—Experiments—Juvenile literature. 2. Climatology—Experiments—Juvenile literature.
[1. Weather—Experiments. 2. Climate—Experiments. 3. Experiments.] I. Title. II. Series.
QC863.5 .W48 2002
551.5'078—dc21

00–013030

Manufactured in the United States of America

Contents

What Makes Weather and Climate

Anytime you go outside, you probably consider the weather without really thinking about it. Is it cold or warm? The day-to-day changes in temperature, wind, and **precipitation**, which includes things like rain, sleet, snow, and hail, are called weather.

Weather is neat because you can see it happening right before your eyes. What we see is the result of layers of air surrounding Earth, called the **atmosphere**, interacting with the land and the oceans. Actually, it is not a single force that creates our weather, but many things working together as a system.

Over time, that system has changed. The patterns in our weather over hundreds or thousands or millions of years are called climate. Scientists study the history of Earth's climate to understand the way our weather works today.

← *Rain, hail, and snow are all types of precipitation.*

See How Earth Stays Warm

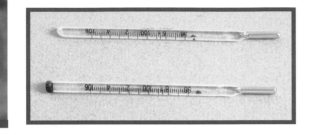

Without an atmosphere, Earth would be a very cold and windy place. Our atmosphere contains different types of **gas**. Carbon dioxide, one of the gases in the atmosphere, lets heat into the planet but doesn't let it out. Tiny drops of water in the atmosphere do the same thing. They let heat reach the planet, then they trap most of it near the surface. This process warms the surface of Earth and makes our weather possible. Without this process, our weather would be very different. Scientists call this process of letting heat in but not out the **greenhouse effect**. You can see the greenhouse effect in action with this simple project.

You will need
- 2 thermometers
- A zip-seal plastic bag big enough to fit one of the thermometers
- A sunny day

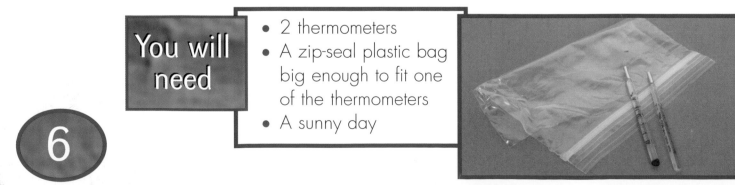

Place one of the thermometers in the plastic bag and seal it.

 On a sunny day, find a spot outside without shade. Put the thermometers next to each other in the sunny spot.

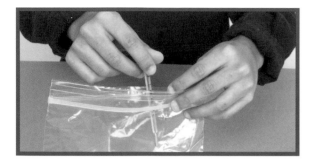

3 Wait 15 minutes.

 4 Read the thermometers. Is one warmer than the other? The thermometer that has been in the plastic bag should have a higher temperature than the one without a bag. The Sun's rays enter the bag and turn into heat, and the heat cannot escape easily. This is just like Earth's atmosphere, which traps heat around the planet.

Track the Air

The air in the atmosphere has a weight that pushes down on us. We call this **air pressure**. How much the air pushes down depends on its temperature. Cold air is heavy and pushes down on us a lot. This is called high pressure. Warm air is light and pushes down on us less. It is called low pressure. Low pressure often means wet weather is coming. High pressure means dry, sunny days. A **barometer** measures this pressure. You can make your own barometer and predict the weather yourself!

You will need

- A 26-ounce (769 ml), wide-mouthed jar
- A 3x5-inch (8x13-cm) index card
- A balloon
- Scissors
- Tape
- A straw
- A rubber band
- A felt-tip pen

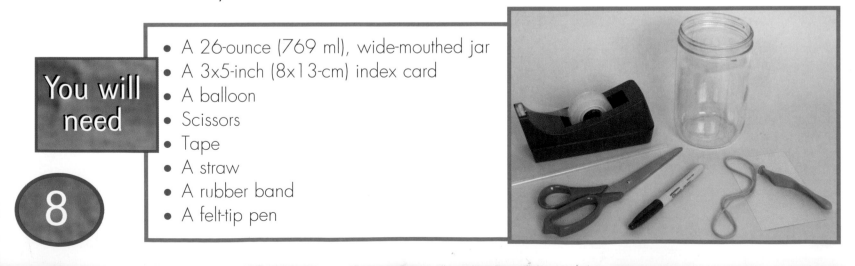

Cut a piece of rubber from a deflated balloon that's big enough to stretch over the mouth of the jar.

 Stretch the piece of balloon tightly over the mouth of the jar and secure it with a rubber band. Make sure no air can get in the jar. Tape the straw to the top of the balloon.

 Draw three lines across the index card about 1 inch (2.5 cm) apart. On the top line write "High," and on the bottom line write "Low."

 Place the jar on a level surface in front of a wall indoors. Tape the card to the wall so that the middle mark lines up with the straw. Check the position of the straw once a day for a week and see if it moves. On cold days, the straw should point toward the "High" pressure line. On warm days, the straw should point toward the "Low" pressure line. If you watch the straw carefully, it will help you predict when the weather is going to change.

Measure the Speed of the Wind

The air that makes up high- and low-pressure systems is constantly moving. Warm air in low-pressure systems rises, and cool air in high-pressure systems sinks. As the air moves around, it creates wind. Strong winds happen when there's a large difference in temperature between two pockets of air. If a really warm patch of air meets a really cool patch, for example, the winds will be strong. You can measure the speed of the wind by using an instrument called an **anemometer**.

You will need

- Five 6-ounce (177-ml) paper cups
- Two drinking straws
- Scissors
- A large sewing needle
- A pencil with an eraser
- A felt tip pen
- Tape
- A 26-ounce (769-ml) container filled with clay, or play dough.

1 Take your pencil and poke four holes near the rim of one of your cups. The holes should all be equal distances apart from one another. Poke another hole in the bottom of the cup.

 2 Using the tip of your scissors, poke a hole through one of your straws at the half-way point on the straw. Ask an adult for help with the scissors. Do the same for the other straw. Slide the straws through the cup's four holes and line up the slits to make an "X."

3 Tape the bottom of one cup to the end of one straw. Tape the other three cups to the other three ends of the straws, making sure the cups all face in the same direction. Use a felt tip pen to make a mark on one of the cups, leaving the other three blank. The colored cup will make it easier to judge the speed of your instrument in the wind.

 4 Carefully push a needle through the center of your straw "X." Poke your pencil through the hole in the bottom of the cup, eraser side up. Now push the needle into the eraser of the pencil, and stick the lead end of the pencil into your container of clay or play dough. You've made an anemometer! Place your anemometer outside. If it's very windy, the cups will twirl quickly. If the wind is weak, they will spin slowly.

Create a Cloud in a Bottle

Water moves around Earth in what is called the **water cycle**. Water falls to Earth as precipitation, filling our lakes, rivers, and oceans. Then it rises into the air, or **evaporates**, to form clouds, only to make more precipitation. **Clouds** are made when tiny drops of evaporated water in the air cool and stick together around bits of dust. These masses of water-covered dust gather together to form clouds. You can produce the conditions needed to form a cloud with this project and create your own cloud in a bottle.

You will need
- A clean, plastic, 2.12-quart (2-liter) soda bottle or juice container
- A sheet of black construction paper
- Clear tape
- Hot water
- Matches
- An adult to help

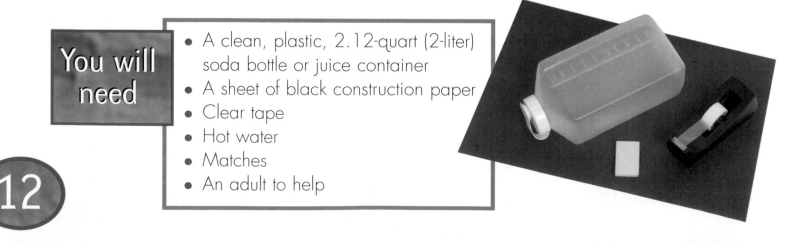

1 Tape the black construction paper to a wall near a flat surface where you can set the bottle and see it easily. The paper will help your cloud be more visible.

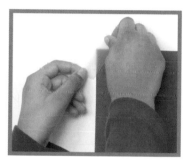

2 Have an adult help you pour about 1 cup (237 ml) of very hot water into the bottle. Blow into the bottle to make sure that it is completely expanded, and put the top on. Shake the bottle for about 1 minute. This will spray tiny particles of water into the air in the bottle, similar to evaporation. Loosen the cap but do not remove it.

3 Ask an adult to light a match. Let it burn for a few seconds, loosen bottle top, quickly put the match in the bottle, and replace the top. The match should be burning when you drop it in the bottle, but it will go out when it hits the water. The smoke makes particles of dust in the air where the water particles can gather.

4 Lay the bottle on its side and push down on the side for about 10 seconds. The pressure should make the water particles stick together, just like cold air. Place the bottle in front of the black paper. Do you see a cloud? Push down again until you see a cloud form. You've made a cloud!

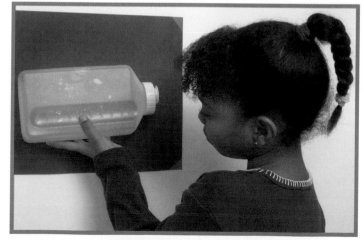

Record the Rain

The tiny water droplets that make clouds can stay in the air as long as they are small and light. When the air cools, the droplets begin to stick together, forming larger and larger drops. When the drops get big enough, they become too heavy to stay in the clouds. They fall to the ground as rain, snow, sleet, or hail. **Gravity**, a force that attracts one object to another, pulls the water drops toward Earth. Depending on where you live, you can measure the amount of precipitation that falls to the ground. Here is one way to measure the amount of rain that falls where you live.

You will need

- An 8-ounce (237-ml), tall, straight cup on which you can write.
- A ruler
- A permanent marker
- Paper and felt tip pen

1 Hold a ruler against the side of the glass. Make sure the bottom of the ruler lines up with the bottom of the glass.

2 Use a permanent marker to draw lines at ¼-inch (about ½-cm) intervals up to the top of the glass. You've made a rain gauge!

3 Place the rain gauge outside on a flat surface. When it rains during the day, go out in the evening and measure the amount of precipitation. Record the date, time, and amount of rain.

4 After you have 5 or 6 measurements, make a chart of the different amounts of rain on different days. Does it change much? Wait a few months and try it again. Does your chart look different?

Make a Climate Timeline

Earth's weather has not always been like it is today. Some periods of history were warmer and some were colder. There have been four major **ice ages**, or times when it was so cold that ice covered parts of the land. Scientists do not totally understand why our climate varies, but they believe it is natural. Today Earth's climate is in a warm spell. Scientists make climate **timelines** so they can better understand how temperatures have changed in the past. Timelines show the order of events in history. You can make your own timeline of Earth's temperature to see how it has changed in the past.

You will need

- 3 different colors of chalk
- A yardstick
- A 25-foot-long (8-m) stretch of sidewalk or pavement on which you can draw.

Find a stretch of sidewalk or pavement that is about 25 feet (8 m) long. At one end draw a square. Color it with the first color of chalk and label it "cold." With a different color of chalk, color another square and label it "warm." The two colors will represent different temperatures.

 Using the third color of chalk, draw a line in front of the squares and mark it "today." Lay the yardstick down so that the end of the stick is on this starting line. With the chalk you used for warm, draw a line the length of the stick. This represents the last 20,000 years of Earth's climate.

 Line up the yardstick with the end of the warm line. With the chalk you used for cold, draw a thick line 3 yardsticks long. This represents the colder climate on Earth between 20,000 and 80,000 years ago.

 Line up the yardstick with the end of the cold line. Draw 3 yardstick lengths with the "warm" chalk. This was another warm period between 80,000 and 140,000 years ago. Then draw one more yardstick length on the end with the "cold" chalk. This was a cold period between 140,000 and 160,000 years ago. Draw a finish line with the third color of chalk. Label this "160,000 years ago."

Create a Clay Core

Most of what scientists know about the history of Earth's climate comes from studying **core samples**. Core samples are layers of ice or dirt pulled up from the ground with long, pipelike tools. Each layer in a core sample equals a certain period of time. Scientists study the chemicals, **fossilized** animals, and tiny rocks in each layer of the core sample to figure out what the weather was like during certain times in the past. By piecing together the weather patterns, they create a history of Earth's climate. With this project, you can find out how to take a core sample and study its layers.

You will need

- 3 different colors of clay, about 2 cups (473 ml) each
- A straw
- A pair of scissors
- An adult to help

18

1 Take 1 cup (237 ml) of a single color of clay and flatten it into a thin pancake. Do the same for each cup of the clay so that you have six thin layers of clay. Try to make them all about the same size.

 2 Place one layer of clay on a flat surface. Lay another color directly on top. Pile on each layer until you have a stack of six clay layers.

 3 Hold the straw over the layers and slowly press it down through the clay until it hits the bottom. Place your finger over the top of the straw and slowly pull it out. Some of the clay should be stuck inside the straw.

 4 Ask an adult to help you cut the straw. Carefully remove the core of clay. Do you see the layers? The layers at the bottom are the oldest because you put them down first. The layers near the top are young because you laid them down last.

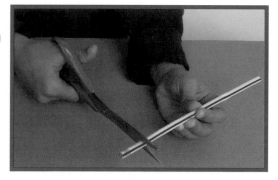

Climate Clues

Each year a tree grows, it forms a new ring of wood just under the bark, called a **growth ring**. During warm years with good weather conditions, the tree gets plenty of food and energy from the Sun and grows wide growth rings. During cold years with harsh weather conditions, the tree does not grow as much, so the rings are small. Over time, the different sizes of growth rings in a tree create a record of Earth's climate. Scientists study tree rings to learn more about the history of Earth's climate in a particular area. You can try it for yourself and make your own tree ring record.

You will need
- A nearby tree stump, piece of firewood, or cut tree
- A ruler
- A magnifying glass
- Paper and pencil

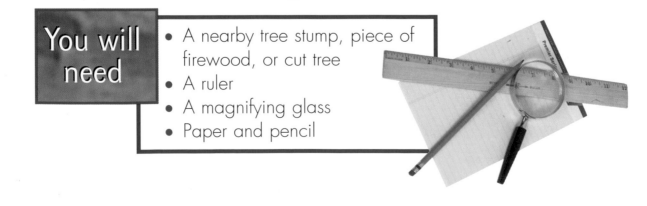

Find a tree stump that is cut flat and is fairly clean. A good place to look is in an empty lot or along a park trail. You need to be able to see the rings inside the tree. If you cannot find a stump, use a piece of firewood with flat ends.

 Using your magnifying glass, count the rings, starting at the outer edge of the tree. Each ring represents one year. The number of rings is the age of the tree. Record the age on your paper.

 For each year of the tree's life, try to decide whether the growth ring is wide or thin. Use your ruler to help you decide. Wide rings indicate a year when the tree grew a lot. This growth could mean the weather was good that year.

 On your paper, for each year of the tree's life, record whether the ring is wide or thin. Now take a look. You have created a rough climate record for that particular tree!

Understanding the Past and the Future

Our weather is constantly changing. This constant change is what makes it so interesting! Weather changes from day to day and from century to century. Scientists have learned that over time Earth's climate has changed a lot. Scientists believe that changes in the position in which Earth travels around the Sun may make our climate change over time, but they are still trying to learn more. If they can understand the history of our climate, they will have a better chance at predicting the future of our weather.

Will coming years be warmer or cooler than in the past? Pay attention to how the weather in your own neighborhood changes from day to day and from year to year. What can you learn?

Glossary

air pressure (EHR PREH-shur) The weight of the atmosphere pushing down on Earth.

anemometer (a-neh-MAH-meh-tur) An instrument used to measure the speed of the wind.

atmosphere (AT-muh-sfeer) The layers of air surrounding Earth.

barometer (beh-RAH-meh-tur) An instrument used to measure air pressure.

clouds (CLOWDZ) Clumps of pressed water drops, or water vapor.

core samples (KOR SAM-pulz) Layers of ice or dirt pulled up from the ground in a cylinder and used to study the history of Earth's climate.

evaporates (ih-VA-puh-rayts) When something is taken into in the air as small pieces.

fossilized (FAH-suh-lyzd) The remains of living things that have turned into rock over time.

gas (GAS) Things that are not liquid or solid and have no shape. This includes oxygen and carbon dioxide.

gravity (GRA-vih-tee) The natural force that attracts one object to another.

greenhouse effect (GREEN-hows eh-FEKT) When gases in the atmosphere let heat into Earth, then trap it near the surface.

growth ring (GROHWTH RING) A layer of wood on a tree that marks growth. One layer stands for one year's worth of growth.

ice ages (EYES AYG-es) Periods of time when ice and glaciers cover parts of the land.

precipitation (prih-sih-pih-TAY-shun) Any form of moisture that falls from the sky, including rain, sleet, snow, and hail.

timelines (TYM-lynz) Schedules of events.

water cycle (WAH-tur SY-kuhl) When water evaporates into the sky, forms clouds, and then falls back to Earth as rain.

Index

Web Sites

To learn more about the weather and climate, check out these Web sites:
www.fi.edu/weather/
www.nws.noaa.gov/
www.ucar.edu/40th/webweather